A Lover's Rapture

Passionate Poetry

By

Maura Burd

authorHOUSE™

1663 LIBERTY DRIVE, SUITE 200
BLOOMINGTON, INDIANA 47403
(800) 839-8640
WWW.AUTHORHOUSE.COM

© 2004 Maura Burd
All Rights Reserved.

First published by AuthorHouse 08/12/04

ISBN: 1-4184-9486-0 (e)
ISBN: 1-4184-9485-2 (sc)

Library of Congress Control Number: 2004096497

Printed in the United States of America
Bloomington, Indiana

This book is printed on acid-free paper.

Book cover image of Helix Nebula ngc7293 courtesy of NASA/STScI.

Table of Contents

Confession to My Lover

I'm in love with your mind

Each fragment of romantic concentration

That you expel upon my spirit

Makes my passion unconfined

In every tender word you whisper expectation

Builds within my desire to submit

To the act of our bodies entwined

In your soft bed of wild inspiration

I will this moment admit!

I'm in love with your mind

Euphoria

I ruminate your heart
Above the summer day
Where silken ribbon
Clouds of white
Do cushion lover's play

In meditation's bliss
We mingle in its foam
Of tranquil velvet
Waterfalls
Desire would never roam

We sprint from lowly seats
Of our exhaustive lives
And dive head first
Engorged confidence
Where ecstasy derives

And down into the depths
Of our illustrious fire
Is where we meet
Sumptuous
Excitements we inspire

Love's Primeval Plea

I merged with you on pleasure shores
Where starlit skies were mine and yours
And dreams were met through secret doors
In splendor shaken winds

You led me through the path of birth
And to the womb that is the earth
Out to the frozen atmosphere of life
Alone and bare

I shan't forget the time of bliss
Of tender touch and rapture's kiss
And only when you pull me back
Will thoughts divine be met

So summon the winds of intervention
Storm on me with one intention
To sever the tie that binds me here
And give my longing rest

The Sound of Your Voice

The sweet taste of remembrance

Dancing starlight upon my view

Drawing in the equivalence

Of our love's reflection and hues

It's the purest form of rapture

Two souls can ever meet

As we're thrust into the core of stature

Our ripe fruits nestle…hidden…discreet

We meld…we whirl on a fragment

Too sapient to possibly fathom

Yet the view is pristine…subliminal

As we rise from out of the chasm

And then I hear your voice…

Oh, its sound just pulls me under!

The quiet roar of infinity

Recalling lifetimes within your thunder

My soul bursts with ecstasy

My thoughts collide with thee!

You weave into my vibration

And engrave me with your decree

Your mark upon my soul is fixed

Your command…my visceral need

I'll live each breath in pause…in wait

For the rush of your voice in me to bleed

Phantom of Dreams

When you touch me

I capitulate

In languid motion

Losing all ability to reach…

To cling

Your hand tugging firmly on my hair

Behind my neck

Demanding my full attention

Makes me swoon in your ferocious care

How strong…

How intense I do long

For your steel blue eyes to burn into mine

Insisting my absolute compliance,

Total submission

Oh, just the thought of you…

Your gaze, your velvet touch,

Your earthy sandalwood scent

I could curl up inside your lascivious fragrance

Eternally, delightfully intoxicated

In your enthralling bliss

Oh, bountiful Phantom…

My desire for you is utmost

My adoration…ultimate

My love…salacious, immortal

Let me never awaken from this dream!

Eros' Kiss

You hide from the tremors of Eros' kiss
Which hovers above Solitude's bed
In shadowy visions he lulls you deep
With the draw of his silken thread

You feel each trace of his transcendent stroke
Ripple the pool of deprivation
That long had kept you in its lonely depths
In search of Love's salvation

In a low voice he whispers, "Come with me."
His vibrations attract you firm in his snare
He draws you deeper into his masterful caress
And ignites you with his seductive flare

Eros comes upon you like wet inspiration
Drenching your valleys of idleness
And binds the thread in you to him
Your soul's pleasure he'll not suppress

Persuasive Guide

You come from golden sand and myrrh
Lapping the sultry winds of time
Across the brazen burning sun
To ravish me on love's bed

Your eyes are pools of topaz streams
That flow and rush upon my vision
In soothing ripples of ecstasy
As all inhibitions shed

I'm thrust into your masculine wind
That whispers across my radiant cheeks
And tender peaks of milky breasts
So firm in you am I embedded

You lure me down on luxurious sheets
That soften my fears beneath your intent
As you close in on me with slow advance
Till you reach my succulent spread

And through the portal of passion's utopia
You gather me into your adagio pace
That binds me to your addictive pleasure
As you channel our connection ahead

Rapture's Passage

I melt…

On your lips

In a silken pocket of raven night

I mingle…

In your arms

To the taut peak of passion's delight

I dance…

On your sword

Like pulsating sanctioned light

We float…

In the wake

Of love's quivering undaunted might

The Pupil

To deny your voice

Would pull me under

It's not its sound

But more its thunder

When you roar my soul

I'm twisted like wheat

Through the fields of want

I am incomplete

My eyes pry open

In your sterling presence

I can see no lechery

Nor false pretense

There's pure rhythm

Between our souls

Of utmost measure

I will extol

My Hunger for You

Feeling the ache...the hunger for you

Across the span of a million miles

Across the vibration of solitary thought

I feel you...

Yet

You're so far away

I can't touch your image

It's distant

Like a future event...destined

Though not yet found

I will reach for you

That you can depend

But still...

I ache for you

I remember our stir

I remember your touch

So skilled...so intense

Oh, how you thrill me!

I will be here

Waiting

For all eternity

If that's what it takes to feel you again

To hear your lapping murmur of desire

Submerging deep into my core

Oh, Lover...

I'm starved for you!

Ravishment of the Maiden

He granted me redemption

When he looked into my eyes

And tore my past transgressions

Out from in to slowly fly

Up to his precipice

Where sun burned out the lies

Of life's ambiguity

And revealed my hungry eyes

That scrutinized him searchingly

Till sight had spread its thighs

Of rigid nonconformity

Unfolding to his rise

Beloved Thief

You sway me down to lay me down

Upon your bed of Yes

I'm taken hostage in your arms

On love's bondage express

You ease me in your hunger's lens

With hopes they'll be no blur

To the depths in which I'll arouse within

Your exhilarating purr

You lure me in to get within

My tender walls of pink

You smother me with velvet paws

And seduce me to the brink

Within your hold I tremble deep

And stand upon the edge

Of seduction's ledge of bittersweet

My desires you probe and dredge

You catch me quick and kiss my lips

To silence my distrust

Then claw me open greedily

And devour me with your lust

Forever will I lavish you

Forever will I please

Upon the bed of your desire

My beloved Prince of Thieves

Birth of the Sage

He journeyed to the peak of his soul's unrest
And focused his perception beyond the precipice
That detained him from sovereignty
And knowledge best
And arrived at the edge of truth

It was there that I found him within the mist
That clouded his vision like a tornadic twist
Of gray debris and puzzlement
And offered my humbleness

With tenacious resolve he funneled through
The storm of illusion that meant to slew
Him back within deception's ruins
But doom would not reign

He floats in tune within the Light
Where wisdom clear is black and white
And pauses not for gaudy deceit
Insight of the Sage gazes on...

Esoteric Wind

The sweet taste of remembrance
Dances lightly upon my view
Drawing in the equivalence
Of our love's reflection subdued

It's the purest form of rapture
That is and will always be
Between the rippling sheets of eternity
In the elation of you and me

No density nor sound nor visual
Can portray the 'hum' of us
The energy flow is recognized
By perception not by ones who discuss

When the cloak of life is blown away
And our two souls converge with peace
We fuse within the ebb and flow
Of tranquility's illuminating release

Poised

Conflicted?

Never!

I know you're he who incites my mystical lust

The man whose sultry gaze I trust

Who impassions me beyond with tempestuous gusts

Afraid?

Never!

I leap into your untamed weeds

Frolicking barefoot through scattering seeds

In your aromatic meadows revealing my creed

Guilty?

Eternally!

I'll stand by you in abominable hell

And in paradisiacal realms where divinity dwells

A fervent devotee forever under your virile spell

Fusion

Render me breathless

Render me soft

Out of rue's prison

Desire soaring aloft

Replace tragic's tears

With warm drops of sweat

Dripping salt from love's forehead

Soaking parched ringlets

Elevate the dark mood that sprawls over the pond

Amend him with fusion

Like an electrostatic bond

And when he's released from his cavernous loft

Bring him here to my chamber

Unleash my feverish soft

Tranquility Stirred

Legs long

Cool

Still

I feel your purpose

Gone the chill

Heat swells within my shell

As you approach

No warning bell

Your needs require my wistful gaze

Redeeming caress

No delays

You seize my silence

Invade me deeper

I'm obeisant!

Oh, ecstasy's keeper

He is There

No one's seen my lover's face

No one

Except for me

He holds my spirit in the forefront

Of life

Invisibly

Illusionists have purloined my attention

Exhibiting ripe fruit

But only He captures my devotion

Ending my eternal pursuit

Wantonness

Float me down your river of quiver
To your causeway of idleness
Submerge me in the pristine depths
Of your rapture's wantonness

Tow me out to your sea of ecstasy
To your infinite arching perspective
Bend me into its gentle curve
That is our soul's connective

Inhale me into your vaporous enclosure
To your prophetic vibrations keep
Then swallow me whole into your monstrous bellows
And squall me with your provocative sweep

Under the Enchanter's Spell

I want to taste every second

Feel every moment

Hear every minute rhythm of his heart

I want to shower him with kisses

Bathe him in romance

Drench him in a sensuous downpour of desire

I want to open my perception

Unlock my longing

Unleash my fervent, signaling fire

I want to attend to his every pleasure

Appear bestowing treasures

Perform in the sanguine dreams he doth inspire

Until I melt into his rhythm

Blend into his colors

And fuse with Immortality's orbiting wire

Return of the Invincible Warrior

There were moments…more like ages
When my life went on…
Uneventful…blue…serene
Then out from the lull of ordinary
Comes my lover…thrust into my scene

His art form is such I can't express
Without sighs…quickening breath
For his sculptured body…ample charm
Does cause my composure sudden death

The knock on my door…from him that day
Gave me pause to turn and run
Reminded of lewd sins before with him
I'd relished…willingly done

But something within me pushed aside
The logic that meant to block
The destined event he meant to deliver
Behind the door he wanted unlocked

And so I breathed my final breath
Then invited my lover inside
His kiss was urgent…his seduction precise
As my thoughts he effortlessly pried

He forged his way into my heart
Claiming sole possession and right
Then locked the door to my escape
And enclosed me on his battlefield of delight

Contact

A flow of salacious energy
Gushes from your deliberate gaze
Of blue green pools of torrid desire
Meant to ignite me...all ablaze

Your disconnected countenance
To most seems innocent
But when you corner me...all alone
You reveal your licentious intent

At first my resistance for you was quick
I'd see you...then promptly I'd hide
But your magnetic intensity has drawn me in
And tonight our bodies will collide

Her Master's Command

Enter my thunder at the edge of time

Where the horizon of life fades into mists sublime

Float above the silken, shimmering winds

And feel the warm pull of my smooth, erotic spin

Fall freely onto the plush bed of my hands

And immerse yourself fully in your lover's hedonic plans

Engage in my kiss as I gnaw upon your lips

In bliss laden thrusts and wet, sensual whips

Drink in my pleasure as it pours over your thirst

And drown in my intensity of lust where you're submersed

Voeux de l'amour

She vows to him…

He cannot steal your elation
Nor trick me into his embrace
For not even a fleeting glimmer
Shall he view from on my face
For it's you whom I give my light
And heave my breasts unto
And it will always be your eyes I melt in
As I ride the deep kiss of you

He vows to her…

So it is with fiendish passion
That I pull you to my chest
And draw you deep within my mouth
Till I swallow your every breath
As it is, you will never escape me
Or be stolen from my jealous keep
For the domination that is my spirit
Shall always connect you to me deep

Dearest

My dearest,

I have seen your shadows in my dreams

Through the long and restless nights

I've awakened at dawn just before its light

In the hopes that you'd be there in my sights

And when your image does not appear

I'm filled again with lonely fright

For I must wait again for thee

To lift me to your love's eternal delight

Mightier than the Sword

You wrote of your lips upon my breast

In morning light's arise from rest

And stirred a hunger deep within

My moist refreshment's tender skin

I cannot wait to feel your touch

Within your arms…within your clutch

Encased within your incessant need

To taste my nectar and proceed

To chamber warmth and velvet thrust

In me your poetry does combust!

Affinity

Stationary water in a boat

A sea upon a sea

Afloat

Dimensions separate yet the same

A symmetry upon a symmetry

Proclaim

Creator and creation exist

A soul upon a soul

Persist

Isolated but one the same

A lover upon a lover

Boundaries…overcame

Enslaved by the Specter

I feel your presence in my house

Somewhere…

You are here

Hiding in an uninhabited room…a dark corner

Unseen, yet deeply do I sense you

I know you are here

I search the perimeters of every room

Scaling the narrow edge of comfort

Peering into the vast darkness surrounding me

Trembling…I close my eyes

Faintly…I call out,

"Are you here?"

Silence…

I hear your beating heart all around me

Drumming its steady rhythm into my eardrums

I begin to fold…

To melt into your trance induced seduction

I open my eyes…silence again

I close my eyes feverishly

Aware that you want my eyes closed

I feel your shadow move in front of me

Then behind me…

Fluttering wildly around me in a fierce storm of desire

I open my eyes

Nothing but my empty room do I see

I close my eyes again

I hear you breathe

My heart pounds with anticipation!

I want to open my eyes…I try

You breathe again

My eyelashes flicker under your excited breath

My eyelids are somehow sealed shut by your mystical power

I attempt to open my eyelids again but fail

I feel you move around me…

Beneath me

I burn for you…ache

Masterfully,

You ease me down onto the floor

I surrender to your need…

My desire pleads for your kiss!

Your amorphous hands trail up and down my body

A firm, yet tender caress of you do I feel

I disrobe…

No!

It's not me removing my clothes

It's you!

Helplessly…longingly,

I sigh as you undress me

I feel your thrilling fingers entwine in mine

You lock me beneath your persuasive presence

Your kiss…your glorious kiss!

Unfathomable desire ignites my soul

"My darling…."

I hear you whisper into my thoughts

I try to speak…wanting to confess my love to you

"Don't speak…feel," you whisper

Then,

Just as undulating currents of love from you surge into me,

A cool shiver moves across my skin

Silence…

I open my eyes

Nothing but my empty room do I see

I close my eyes

And receive your forewarning,

"Tomorrow night," you say,

As it's been since the first night you haunted me

And will remain to be for the rest of my eternity,

"I will return…"

Your warning shakes every fragment of my being

You hold my chin up firmly…demanding full attention

You then add,

"I will have you, Lover…again…."

Neptune's Mistress

I saw the glint within his eyes

An amber glow…a lilting reprise

And when he lulled me to him near

I saw a valiant, unscrupulous revere

That made me awestruck by his intent

Which he'd both showcase and circumvent

And so I fell at Neptune's feet

A drowning victim…his thirst complete

Rogue

Misbehave

And have your way

This custom of yours

Oh, illustrious knave

Makes ruby lips

Lie in wait

For your masculine scent

To permeate

So when you whisper

In sensuous voice,

"What do you think?

Would you deeply rejoice?"

I'll take a breath…

Fall right in

I'm a woman who can't

Resist your grin

Omniscient Lover

I was drawn inside

Your infinite omniscience

And enveloped by obscure silhouettes

That fueled my need to lay in the sway

Of your hallowed, demonstrative nets

The stroke of your brush

Painted me azure

As I capitulated beneath your wind

That caressed the chambers of my insatiable needs

Arousing original sin

Hold back nothing

From you, will I

As I bathe you with kisses of explicit content

As we linger in the quivering of our gypsy fire

And never shall we repent!

More!

I want to taste every second

Feel every moment

Hear every minute rhythm of your heart

You want to shower me with kisses

Bathe me in romance

Drench me in a sensuous downpour of desire

We want to open our perception

Unlock our longing

Unleash our fervent, signaling fires

We want…more!

Immortal Legacy

How can I ignore you, majestic sentinel of my soul,

When out of the corner of my eye you're always present

Watching me with absolute concentration…

Licking your lips…salivating

Waiting for me to look into your voracious, haunting eyes

I know that when I do crawl helplessly into your gaze

As you desire…as you intend,

Even if it is out of mesmeric curiosity

It will be my mortal death

This is my inheritance…my bloodline's fate

Like time,

Our immortal connection will tell

It's only a matter of breaths now for the destined encounter to occur

The very act that changes my existence and yours

There is no escape

Even as I wake at dawn

I feel the swing of the pendulum lull me further into your pulse

The sunlight streaming in my window invades me…burns me

I pull the shades closed

Sealing out the light of day that wants to keep me here

And I wait

I lie in bed this night

My heart pounds with profuse anticipation

Out of the corner of my eye I notice your form beside me

Unafraid, I turn my head towards you

You emerge from the shadows…boldly… invincibly

I see you clearly now…as you are

Beautiful…descended angel from the netherworld

Your dark, hypnotic eyes penetrate me

I rise freely to you…floating…weightless as a vibration

Your bite on my soul is the most sincere pain I've ever known

Please, never unclench your bite on me!

Tear me!

Rip me into tender shreds of pure pleasure!

Like this fateful night's arrival,

I've hungered eternally for you, my Immortal Master

You've seized me from the life of shadows

That had long toyed with my perception

I am engulfed,

Enflamed by your arousing kiss as you transport me

Eternally…

Into the netherworld with you

Where all consuming love and passion sustains our souls

I pause exquisitely in our reflection…

For you…for us…for the harmonious radiance of our bond

The relentless swing of the pendulum has finally stopped

Mortal life ticks no more

Rhapsody's Maestro

Beneath the resonation of my subtle harp
Exists the torrid rumble of your bass
Polarizing me helpless with intricacy
Upon the jagged barb of your sensual pace

You impale me profound and powerfully
And maneuver me up, face to face
Guiding me through your passion's crescendo
To the moistness of your breathing space

This movement of indulgence between our strings
Propels me illicitly, far from grace
I'm absorbed, my Maestro, into your symphony
An orchestral nymph in your compelling chase

The Birdbath

I spread my wings of brown and white
And circle the dell where lives my love
A cruel visitor I'm thought at sight
From ones who curse beasts from above

To see you walk in the day by the river
Where I hunt for morsels and drink
Sends my flight on a frolicking quiver
As I watch you dream, write and think

Oh, if I could tell you, my darling man
That I, a hawk, am full enchanted
By the lush depth within your span
Could you, please…my wish be granted?

But I fear at once if our eyes do meet
You'll scorn me because of my infamy
And run for cover on cautious feet
To your safe shanty beneath the tree

You'd plot to kill the winged beast
That soared like a menacing threat
About to claw your eyes for a feast
In a defeat your pride could not forget

And so I'll adore from high above
As my man does dream, write and think
And long for the day when I bathe my love
In him where I'll drift, float and sink

Physique of the Mystic

He met me in sunlight,

So dazzling, by the fountain

Pondering my spirit

As he peered into my soul

I sat down beside him

And listened intently

As he prophesized on reason

And the significance of his role

I couldn't get past his desirable lips

That moved so eloquently

With each theory he expressed

And when he suggested

I accept his philosophy

I could only wish his lips on my breasts

He leaned in closer

When my silence was given

Thinking me frozen in suspense

But when I placed my hand in his

He winked his line of defense,

"The touch of your hand

Reminds me of something

So sweet…and oh…so wet

Like sun warmed mango

Sliding across my tongue

73

In me a fierce hunger is now beset

Your eyes they glisten,"

He then prophesized,

"Like heavenly stars I must invade

But oh, your lips,

My precious one,

I ache to kiss and serenade."

I followed the Mystic

Into his secret chamber

Bathed in wisdom and cosmic dust

And opened my mind

To the Mystic's glories

And gave him my utmost trust

We studied the universe

Within our eyes

And practiced the laws of nature

And when he continued

With my intimate lesson

He envisioned my soul in his future

A thousand years

Have past since then

That day when first we met

And still my love

For him does flow

Upon the lips of the Mystic's silhouette

Psyche's Reverie

In what dream of mine did you first arrive?
In what forbidden Eden did we kiss?
Where the rose petal's blush and dew drenched leaves
Held us…lush…within its ambrosial midst

The twinkling starlight that bathed our eyes,
From what remote galaxy was it beamed?
Oh, never has my essence yearned so deep
For an existence I'd only dreamed

Tonight when the darkness fills my room
And the mantle of sleep absorbs my will,
We'll meet…luxuriant…in our secret Eden
Evoked into Love's enigmatic thrill

The Alchemist

He gave me a token of his affection

It was the manna of his heart

Placed into my hand

I watched it glisten upon my palm…a prism of light

He raised my hand until its scent seeped into my vision

Our spirits embraced as bass sensations emerged

Melding us together

It was the secret of his love

Whispered into my thoughts

His brew of pleasure injected me into his prism

The flickering heat from his domain now caresses me

He sweeps over my desire like hot desert wind

That I cannot escape…nor do I want to escape

Connecting me to him

It is the tantric power of his divinity

Thrust into my soul

I am bottled eternally inside his translucent prism

A pleasure he diligently, deliberately devised

I am his erotic perfume…capped only for him

Your Kiss

Sandalwood

Umber

Warm musk

Shadowy visions of white jasmine at dusk

Smooth

Rich

The afterglow

Your eyes lurid pools of passion's flow

Strength

Brawn

Sweltry steel

Visual delight your stiff appeal

Swept

Carried

Ravished sweet

Within your arms I feel replete

Bow

Lay

Open wide

I give vigilance upon your slide

Flow

Free

Wistful bliss

There is none wetter than your bottomless kiss

Beyond the Threshold

Your insight…seductive

Your philosophy…inducible

Your caress…my wading pool

I wandered into your garden seeking only rest

Upon resting…a revelation

A showering of brilliant orbs of delights fell upon me

Reviving my composure with verve

I look in your eyes

I'm enchanted

Your intensity…addictive

Your charisma…magnetic

Your power…invincible

I'm unworthy to be in your garden of such perfect splendor

I want to bow down to you…surrender my life, my soul

You move in closer

Closer

Deeper into my consciousness

I tremble

I fear you'll reach your destination in me

You whisper, "There is no end…."

About the Author

Maura Burd is a published romance writer of short story and poetry. Her publications include her books; a paranormal romance collection *White Light Parallel 8 Stories of Love*, a romantic poetry collection *A Lover's Whisper*, and a passionate poetry collection *A Lover's Rapture;* all three books published by AuthorHouse.

Previous poetry publications as part of an anthology include *Touch* in Poetic Voices and *Of Being a Dreamer* in Treasured Poems of America; Sparrowgrass Poetry Forum.

She received the Golden Poet award for her poetry from World of Poetry and is a member of Romance Writers of America.

Maura resides in Pennsylvania with her husband Randell and their dog.

For more information on Maura, visit her website at **www.mauraburd.com**

Printed in the United States
31518LVS00001BA/208